The Indispensable Survival Guide To Ontario's Long-Term Care System

Practical Tips To Help You And Your Family Be Proactive And Prepared

Karen Cumming   Patricia Milne

Tellwell Talent
www.tellwell.ca

ISBN
978-0-2288-2091-8 (Paperback)
978-0-2288-2092-5 (eBook)

This book is dedicated to our dear mother,
Verna Amelia Cumming.

We called her "The Queen".

She taught her family to embrace
the end of life with grace,
humour and dignity.

Mom, you live in our hearts now and forever.

Table of Contents

PREFACE

"But it is a long way to the Emerald City… you must pass through rough and dangerous places before you reach the end of your journey."

—L. Frank Baum,
The Wonderful Wizard of Oz

PREFACE

"But it is a long way to the Emerald City... you must pass through rough and dangerous places before you reach the end of your journey."

—L. Frank Baum,
The Wonderful Wizard of Oz

Remember *The Wonderful Wizard of Oz*? Of course, you do. It's the story of a girl who goes on a journey to a place she's never been before. Bad things happen. Good things happen. In the end, she learns the lessons she needs to know about life and love and about herself.

Sound familiar?

Just like Dorothy, you too are about to go on a journey. Except you're not heading to the land of Oz. You're following the yellow brick road into the deep dark wilds of Ontario's long-term care system.

Perhaps you're helping your elderly parent. Perhaps you're on the journey yourself. Whatever the case, you'll have a feeling you're not in Kansas anymore. You'll be dodging wicked witches, flying monkeys and munchkins at every turn. You may even want to run home to Auntie Em and Uncle Henry. We wouldn't blame you if you did.

Here's the good news. It's all going to be okay.

Consider this little book your survival guide for the journey you're about to take.

We're not going to lie. The long-term care system can be a scary place. Unless you work in healthcare or know someone who does, you've probably never had much to do with it before. One day, you just woke up and realized that your aging mother or father could no longer live in their home alone. Maybe they were staying in an assisted living facility and suddenly couldn't walk anymore. Maybe they were hit by a crisis of a different kind.

It's one of those moments that Oprah loves to talk about. The lightbulb went on above your head. The penny dropped. You understood in a deeper way than you ever did before that your mom or dad would need a higher level of care than their current home could provide.

You're not alone. Hundreds of thousands of baby boomers across Ontario are in the same boat. There are more than 2.4 million people aged 65 and older living in this province as of late 2019.[1] Some are the caregivers; some are the cared-for.

We wrote this for all of you. It's the survival guide we never had.

This book found its beginnings as a feature article appearing in the *Hamilton Spectator*, the *St. Catharines Standard* and the *Peterborough Examiner* in May of 2019. In it, we chronicled our mother's journey through the long-term care system and the roller coaster ride that it became for our family. We suggested at the end of the article that we were working on an e-book. The response from readers was swift and heartfelt. They encouraged us to get it done and to get it out into the world.

We're doing this for one reason. We have been where you are now.

And we would have given our right arm for someone to have guided us through the system – a confusing maze of care coordinators, nurses, doctors, PSWs,

---

[1] Statistics Canada. Table 17-10-0005-01 Population estimates on July 1st, by age and sex https://www150.statcan.gc.ca/t1/tbl1/en/tv.action?pid=1710000501

assessments, occupational therapists, paperwork, equipment rentals, medications… and the list goes on.

It felt like the only people who spoke the mysterious language of long-term care were those on the inside of the system. It was all Greek to us. Literally. We were outsiders – tourists in a foreign land trying to find the Parthenon without a map.

There were times when we thought we would lose our minds.

Even now, we find it hard to believe. No one took us under their wing in meaningful way. No one gave us a colourful brochure that explained all the basics. No one gave us the one-on-one coaching that we needed… that everyone needs.

It didn't take us long to realize that we'd have to coach ourselves, learn the ins and outs of the system, and advocate for our mother like never before. With the help of a spiral bound notebook and a ballpoint pen, we wrote down everything… every conversation, every contact, every phone number and every personal reflection we had time for. We ate, we slept, we asked hundreds of questions and we tore out our hair. During whatever time was left, we vowed to be there for our Mom.

We also vowed that one day, we'd be there for other families who were on the same journey.

It's a life experience that all of us as human beings will go through, but the harsh reality is that few of us are truly prepared. Our hope is that this book will change all of that.

Your Indispensable Survival Guide features:

- Easy-to-understand language
- Information on the basics of the LHIN (local health integration network) and long-term care systems
- Links that take you directly to the resources you need on LHIN and other government websites
- Advice on researching homes and compiling your list of preferred facilities
- Guidance on what to do after a long-term care bed is offered
- Practical tips on buying essentials, adaptive clothing and assistive devices
- Additional insights into life in long-term care
- Dozens of survival tips
- Little-known details that the system simply does not educate us about

Our deep desire is to leave you as prepared as humanly possible to make the decisions for your parent that lie ahead… much more prepared than we ever were.

Think of us as Glinda, the Good Witch of the North. We have a magic wand, and we're here to wave it over you every step of the way.

So put on your ruby slippers, Dorothy. Let's do this.

Karen Cumming & Patricia Milne

Authors' Note: We wish to acknowledge that everyone's journey down this yellow brick road is unique. You may be having a wonderful experience with Ontario's long-term care system. If that's the case, we're truly happy to hear it. But in the event that you're struggling to preserve your sanity – as we were – *we've got your back.*

INTRODUCTION: Love Yourself

"Love is the cure."

—Rumi

INTRODUCTION: Love Yourself

"Love is the cure."

—Rumi

A journalist friend of ours whose stepfather may soon be heading into long-term care recently shared her frustrations with us.

> I'm a resourceful person, and I'm having trouble figuring this out. What about people who don't have those skills? What about the elderly who have no friends or family to advocate for them? What about baby boomers who are so busy with kids, grandkids and jobs that they don't have time to go to the bathroom, never mind care for their elderly mom or dad?

Boy, can we relate.

We said exactly the same thing to ourselves more than once. We were resourceful, too. And yet the system tested our mettle every step of the way. Even a daily meditation and mindfulness practice couldn't keep us from flipping out once in a while and shaking our fists at the sky.

Our friend's story came as a real wake-up call. How many people out there might need help on this journey? As it turns out, more than we imagined.

Our dear mom, Verna, began *her* journey into the final few months of her life in the fall of 2018. With each passing day, we felt more and more frustrated. Doctors, nurses, PSWs and LHIN staff all appeared to be in their own "silo". They were the key players in the system, but they didn't seem to communicate with each other, or with us, very much.

Some days, we just felt powerless. It was as if we were trying to canoe across the Atlantic without a paddle. We laughed about it as often as we could, but in actual fact, we found it frightening.

Truth be told, there'll most likely be times when you'll feel powerless, too. You'll have no idea what to do or which way to turn. Every road you go down will feel like a dead end. Every bureaucrat you call will give you the number of another bureaucrat who may not answer the phone.

You'll leave messages that are never returned. You'll want to give up multiple times a week. You'll buy twice as many lottery tickets as usual so that you might win it big, move your mom or dad into posh private care, and forget all about the public system.

Take it from us... *Love yourself.*

You must make your mental health a priority on this journey. It will make all the difference. Keep your cool. Keep it together. Keep your stick on the ice, as that great Canadian philosopher, Red Green, would say.

You may not know it now, but love and self-care will be your saviours. The first rule of survival is to take care of YOU so that you can take care of your parent when they need you most. Here are some simple strategies to help you show yourself a little love whenever you need it:

- Before you get out of bed in the morning, close your eyes and focus on your breath for 60 seconds. You'll be amazed at how this daily practice will help you to quiet your mind.
- With your eyes still closed, visualize your day unfolding in the best possible way... the

errands you need to run, the conversations you need to have, the tasks you need to complete. Then get out of bed and step into that vision.

- No matter how much is going wrong, something is always going right. Train your brain to focus on what's good.
- Congratulate yourself on the little victories. There will be many.
- Hang on to your sense of humour no matter what.
- Laugh whenever you can and keep your mom or dad laughing, too. It's so important for their mental health and yours.
- Have a debrief session each night with a family member or trusted friend – in person or on the phone. Get the frustrations of the day off your chest and put them in the past so that you can start fresh tomorrow.

Some days will be long; some will be frustrating. In no particular order, you may feel overwhelmed, exasperated and exhausted. Love yourself, keep your mental health top of mind, and the best possible version of you will show up for your mom or dad each day.

You can do this. Yes. You. Can.

Survival Tip:

Love and self-care aren't the only things that will support your mental health on this journey. Being organized will, too. Take a few minutes now to skim through the rest of this guide before you continue reading. Familiarize yourself with the links that are sprinkled throughout. They'll lead you to a wide variety of truly helpful resources quickly and efficiently. They'll save you time. They'll save you energy. They'll help you hang on to your sanity.

Readers of the print edition of this guide will find it essential to consult our webpage, where we've collected all of these links in one central location, listed by page number. Accessing the links online will save you from having to enter sometimes long URLs into your browser manually. Check for updates to these links from one edition of the book to the next. You'll find our webpage at: **indispensableguide.ca**

Ask Great Questions

"The important thing is to not stop questioning."

—Albert Einstein

1

Ask Great Questions

"The important thing is to not stop questioning."

—Albert Einstein

Remember the seventies detective show *Columbo*? Now there was a guy who knew how to ask great questions. He'd show up at the scene of a murder in his rumpled raincoat, take a puff on his cigar, wrinkle his brow, and bam! That's when he'd nail the suspect with a great question they just weren't expecting.

"Why was your wife on the boat that night if she couldn't swim?"

The crook would stutter and stammer, but Columbo was the master. He kept the questions coming until the villain broke down and confessed.

If you want to survive your journey through the long-term care system, you need to start asking great questions. There were times when we felt just like Columbo. Some of our questions made people uncomfortable. We didn't care. We waited as long as we had to for the answers we needed to hear.

It was a pretty successful strategy – one that we encourage you to use.

Look at it this way. Your tax dollars are paying the salaries of the people inside the long-term care system. You're the boss and the customer all rolled into one. *It's their job to help you.*

Part of the reason we got so good at asking questions was that we were completely clueless. We knew nothing about the way the system worked. Nothing. There was no option; we had to be Columbo.

Happily, you can become good at asking questions, too. Whether you're meeting with your parent's doctor, talking to the care coordinator, or consulting with your mom or dad's nurse or personal support worker (PSW), these tips will help you to *ask with ease*:

- Before you start the conversation, write down your questions in a special notebook dedicated to your parent's care. We called ours the *Book of Verna*. It became our diary for every meeting and phone call. We recorded the date, the person we spoke with, the topic of conversation, and any next steps required. It was a godsend.

- Leave space between each question in order to take notes. Don't trust your memory; ours was unreliable at best. These notes will be a lifesaver when you need to recall the details later on.

- Understand that documenting conversations is part of your job as a caregiver. We were amazed at how easily we forgot the fine details of discussions we had had only a day or two before. Once we started keeping notes in our diary, everything changed. We felt organized. We had a resource that we could consult whenever we needed it. As an added bonus, on those days when one of us couldn't be with Mom, reading the notebook the next time we were there was a way of catching up on the latest developments.

- Feel free to say, "I don't understand." These are powerful words. Healthcare professionals often use medical or bureaucratic jargon without realizing that it's a foreign language to those of us on the outside of the system. Try something like: "Could you please explain that to me in a way that might be easier to understand?" (*See below.)

- Take your time. Don't allow anyone to rush you through a meeting.
- If you'd prefer, ask a friend to come with you and take notes so that you can focus on the discussion.
- No friend available? Consider recording the meeting on your phone – with permission, of course – and listening to it afterwards in order to make notes yourself.

The bottom line? Get used to asking great questions. And while you're at it, get used to questioning authority in general when it's necessary.

Be calm, be considerate, be polite, but question.

It was our experience that employees inside the system were sometimes surprised when we did this. At the end of the day, you have every right to question your parent's care and to keep doing so until you get answers that make sense to you.

Survival Tip:

*Healthcare professionals and bureaucrats like to use acronyms in conversation. They're often unaware that we have no idea what they're talking about. For example, the government program designed to help families pay for assistive devices like wheelchairs and walkers is called the "Assistive Devices Program." Your parent's occupational therapist will likely call it the ADP. "Ontario Health Teams" are known as OHTs. "Alternate level of care" translates as ALC. "Do not resuscitate" is routinely referred to as DNR. "Power of Attorney" is POA. These are just a few of many. The bottom line? Know your acronyms. If you don't understand what one of these abbreviations means, don't hesitate to ask for an explanation.

Keep It Simple: The Basics

"Life is really simple, but we insist on making it complicated."

—Confucius

2

Keep It Simple: The Basics

"Life is really simple, but we insist on
making it complicated."

—Confucius

Confucius really knew what he was talking about.
Life should be simple. Unfortunately, the long-term
care system often seems to go out of its way to make
things complicated. In our view, the people in charge
rarely seem to communicate information in a way that
is user-friendly… whether in person, on the phone, or
on a government website. As caregivers, we just want
to have basic info at our fingertips to help us along the
path. It doesn't feel like too much to ask.

Our mission is to make things simple for you.

So get ready to cover the basics in the easiest possible
way – starting with the most basic question of all:

How does the long-term care system work?

If you're anything like we were, you have no idea. The first thing we suggest is that you check out this page on the Ontario government's **Ontario.ca** website. It will give you a brief (and we mean brief) overview of the system. If you don't know a thing about it, this is a good start.

https://www.ontario.ca/page/about-long-term-care

How does the placement process work?

As it turns out, our Hamilton Niagara Haldimand Brant LHIN has a PDF guide to long-term care placement available on the home page of its website (see link below). If you scroll to the bottom of the page and click on **Long-Term Care**, the PDF will download automatically.

http://www.hnhblhin.on.ca/

(Curiously, this does not mean that all LHINs offer the same PDF guide. For some reason, each local health integration network designs its own website and decides what resources it will or will not offer regardless of what the other LHINs are doing. Google the name of your LHIN and "long-term care placement PDF" in order to find the guide for your geographic area. There may be areas where it's simply unavailable.)

We had no idea that either of these resources existed. We only discovered them after our mother had passed away. Both would have been helpful. Again, a disappointing lack of communication between the LHIN and our family.

How much does it cost for basic, semi-private and private accommodation?

Take a look at the page below... another page we had no idea existed. It gives you the costs of different kinds of beds in a long-term care facility: basic, semi-private and private. (More on the difference between those types of accommodation later.) It also has some of the details on government subsidies, if your parent needs help to pay for their care in basic 4-bed accommodation.

https://www.ontario.ca/page/get-help-paying-long-term-care

Channelling your inner Columbo yet? Good! Here are some more great questions:

What the heck is a LHIN?

When our mother Verna first needed the services of the LHIN a decade or more ago following cancer treatment, we didn't even know what the letters L-H-I-N stood for. That should have been our wake-up call right then and there. If we didn't know what a LHIN was, how could we possibly know what it was supposed to do to help us?

We were a couple of deer in the headlights. Really.

As it turns out, LHIN stands for Local Health Integration Network. In 2006, the Local Health Integration Act divided the province into 14 regions and established 14 separate LHINs. They each began assuming their role in managing local health services in April of 2007.[2]

LHINs plan, fund and integrate health services. They're responsible for long-term care homes, home and community care services, public and private hospitals, community support service organizations, mental health and addiction agencies, and community health centres.[3]

The LHIN staff in each region are considered a "point of access" between you and Ontario's home and community care system. Think of them as the middleman who gets your mom or dad from wherever they are now – to wherever they need to go in the community.

---

[2] Auditor General's Report, 2015 http://www.auditor.on.ca/en/reports_en/en15/3.08en15.pdf
[3] Service Ontario, August 2019

What is the home and community care system?

Home care refers to care that your elderly parent may receive in their own home from personal support workers (PSWs), nurses, physiotherapists, occupational therapists, etc.

Community care refers to care that your parent may receive in facilities in the community – for example, a hospital, a supportive housing/assisted living facility or a long-term care home.

When do I need to contact the LHIN?

If you're brand new to the LHIN system, here are three general scenarios you may find yourself in with your elderly parent... scenarios that will require you to call and make an appointment with a care coordinator.

Scenario One

Your mom or dad may still be living at home and need help with bathing, dressing or light housework.

A care coordinator will visit, do an assessment, and determine whether personal support care – paid for by the government – might be provided, and if so, how often.

After cancer treatment more than 10 years ago, our mother was lucky enough to receive a PSW seven days a week in her own home. You'd likely be hard pressed to find anyone that fortunate now. It's common knowledge that there is a severe shortage of PSWs in the province at this point in time.

The President of the Ontario Personal Support Workers Association, Miranda Ferrier, calls it "a crisis."[4] With huge numbers of seniors requiring care, supply just isn't keeping up with demand. A recent survey by the association indicates that personal support worker is not a profession of choice these days, due to such issues as burnout, pay, unsafe work environments and long, often unpredictable hours.[5]

Depending on the LHIN's assessment, you may have to arrange private PSW care for your parent to make up for whatever the province cannot provide. (See the Appendix for tips on hiring a private PSW.)

Scenario Two

Your parent may decide that they can no longer handle living in their own home and that it's time to move into supportive housing – also known as assisted living.

---

[4]   Hamiltonnews.com, November 28, 2018 https://www.hamiltonnews.com/community-story/9055824-lack-of-personal-support-workers-affects-local-home-care-and-long-term-care/

[5]   Ibid.

A care coordinator will assess your parent and verify whether they are eligible. It will then be up to you to research a facility that your mom or dad would like to move into. If there is a vacancy, you will submit your application through your care coordinator. If there is a waiting list, your parent's name will be added to it.

What services will be provided in supportive housing? First and foremost, your mom or dad will receive help with dressing and bathing. Their meals will be prepared for them, their laundry will be done for them, and they'll have access to a variety of recreational activities – including exercise classes.

One thing you need to know about supportive housing is that it is governed by the Residential Tenancies Act. Your mom or dad will be renting a suite in a facility – much like we might rent an apartment. Despite the fact that they are receiving services from the facility, the management has nothing to do with their medical care. Nothing. It's a small point, but an important one to understand.

Management also has nothing to do with settling complaints or arguments between residents. This took us by surprise. We didn't discover this until several years after our mother had moved into supportive housing. Mom wanted to complain about the behaviour of another resident.

We were told there was nothing that the home could do. As long as the woman paid her fees on time, she was technically a tenant in good standing and couldn't be disciplined. Again, a small point, but an important one to know.

Assisted Living Search Tips

If assisted living is your destination for the moment, ask your care coordinator for a printed list of the available choices. If he or she directs you to the internet to find it for yourself, insist on a printed copy and/or ask them to email you a direct link to the list online. Finding the page yourself without guidance is an exercise in frustration.

All that being said, if you're feeling brave enough to give it a try, check out this shortcut:

Google the website "www.healthline.ca" and the name of your LHIN in the same search window. If you don't know the name of your LHIN, call the government helpline 2-1-1 and ask the operator for assistance. We live in the Hamilton Niagara Haldimand Brant LHIN, so Google tells us to go to **www.hnhbhealthline.ca**

Take a look at the map in the top right corner. Click on your region.

This will take you to a page that gives you the option to click on **Supportive Housing**. Do that and enter your postal code in the search window at the bottom.

> You will now be taken to a page that lists all of the supportive housing (or assisted living) facilities within 20 kilometres of your postal code.
>
> Click on any one of them for more information and to book a tour.

Scenario Three

Your parent may be living at home or in supportive housing and needs to get on the waiting list for long-term care. This was our mother's situation.

A LHIN care coordinator will assess your parent and determine whether or not they may be in enough distress to be considered a "crisis case." If your mom or dad is bedridden and/or can no longer walk on their own, for example, they cannot continue to stay in supportive housing. The PSWs there are not permitted to help a resident walk.

At this point, the care coordinator will ask you to compile your list of preferred long-term care facilities. If your parent is deemed a crisis case, they will go on the "crisis list" and will be pushed to the top of the general waiting list. The idea is to get them into long-term care as soon as possible for their own safety and wellbeing. Much more on this process in Chapter 4.

First, let's answer some more great questions.

What happens if my parent is currently in hospital and needs admission to long-term care?

If your mom or dad goes to hospital, receives treatment, recovers, but then needs long-term care, the rules say they cannot go directly from a hospital bed to a long-term care bed. They must transfer to an ALC or *alternate level of care* bed inside the hospital – or to a transitional bed in a nearby retirement home – while they wait for accommodation in one of their preferred long-term care homes.

As it turns out, hospitals only have so many beds allotted for alternate level of care. We've been told informally that LHIN staff are now doing what they can to cut down on the use of ALC beds in order to make those beds available – as frequently as possible – to hospital patients.

That means that more seniors are being assigned to transitional beds in other facilities, and that brings its own set of concerns. Among them, the issue of *secure units*. Secure units are locked to keep patients with dementia and behavioural issues from running off. As luck would have it, transitional beds are sometimes most available in these units.

Imagine how frustrating it is for patients of sound mind to be assigned to a secure unit. That's exactly what happened to a friend of ours. (Read her story in the next chapter.)

What the heck is a super agency?

No story would be complete without a plot twist, right? Here it is.

Ten days after our mother's passing in February of 2019, the Ford government announced big changes to the healthcare system in Ontario. A super agency called Ontario Health is in the works – one that will see the LHINs dissolved. You read correctly: dissolved.

The plan calls for the duties of the LHINs to be merged with those of six existing provincial healthcare agencies. Some of them you may recognize; some of them you may not. You've probably heard of Cancer Care Ontario and eHealth Ontario. Also on the list are the Trillium Gift of Life Network, Health Shared Services, Health Quality Ontario, and HealthForce Ontario.

Confused? Join the club. Why is all of this happening? The province's Minister of Health, Christine Elliott, put it this way:

> The reason why we're doing this – and
> it is a transformational change – is to
> centre care around patients, families and

caregivers. That's not happening now. And
we want to truly integrate and connect
their care so that patients have a seamless
experience throughout their care journey
and throughout their lives.[6]

Will this government truly be able to provide a
"seamless experience" for long-term care patients? For
any kind of patients? Heaven only knows. We can tell
you that our mother did not have a seamless experience
throughout her long-term care journey, and we know
that she isn't the only one. We've met a number of baby
boomer families who have struggled inside the system
as much as we did.

How will the super agency work?

Christine Elliott says that healthcare will continue to be
delivered locally by regional groups known as OHTs or
Ontario Health Teams. She suggests these collaborative
groups of healthcare workers will guide patients from
one care provider to the next and "…would take the
guesswork out of navigating the healthcare system."[7]

The OHTs are expected to be made up of hospitals,
homecare providers, long-term care placement workers,
doctors, social workers, mental health workers, and

---

[6] cbc.ca, February 26, 2019 https://www.cbc.ca/news/canada/toronto/
doug-ford-ontario-health-super-agency-lhin-cancer-care-1.5032830
[7] Ibid.

more. The government was initially planning on thirty to fifty teams throughout Ontario but has received so many applications that it is re-thinking those numbers.[8]

So here's the million dollar question: Will this setup be any more effective than the one we have now? Elliott admits it will take years for the new system to "become mature."[9] In our view, that doesn't bode well for the future. This big new healthcare machine will have lots of moving parts. We won't be at all surprised if the plan doesn't come together as quickly or efficiently as the politicians would have us believe.

The Ontario Nurses Association calls the super agency plan "a prescription for disaster."[10] The Ontario Public Service Employees Union, which represents tens of thousands of frontline healthcare workers, calls it Premier Doug Ford's "ultimate betrayal."[11] You'll have your own opinions.

---

[8] Details of the Super Agency plan are contained in new legislation known as "The People's Health Care Act, 2019". https://www.ola.org/sites/default/files/node-files/bill/document/pdf/2019/2019-04/b074ra_e.pdf

[9] Canadian Healthcare Technology, February 27, 2019 https://www.canhealth.com/2019/02/27/ontario-reorganizes-delivery-of-care/

[10] Ontario Health Coalition, July 25, 2019 https://www.ontariohealthcoalition.ca/index.php/how-ontarios-new-regional-health-teams-will-operate-is-anyones-guess-in-low-rules-environment/

[11] OPSEU News, February 26, 2019 https://opseu.org/news/health-care-super-agency-fords-ultimate-betrayal-opseu-president-thomas

For the moment, we can only deal with what's in front of us, and for better or worse, that is the LHIN system. As that system continues to evolve, however, be sure to check our website regularly for updates on the latest developments.

Survival Tip:

Invest some time to learn how both the healthcare system and the long-term care system work. As your journey progresses, these fundamentals will be your friend. Believe it.

Proactive and Prepared

"By failing to prepare, you are preparing to fail."

—Benjamin Franklin

3

Proactive and Prepared

"By failing to prepare, you are preparing to fail."

—Benjamin Franklin

Benjamin Franklin said it, and so did the Boy Scouts. Be prepared.

The reason most of us aren't prepared, of course, is that we tell ourselves we don't have time. Curiously, we seem to be able to make time for things that are important to us: planning a wedding, planning a vacation, researching a new car.

We need to change our mindset.

Once we realize that planning our mom or dad's long-term care is an equally important life event, we'll start making it a priority. We'll start doing our homework. We'll start to become proactive and prepared.

Since our journey began, we've heard multiple stories of people and their parents drowning in red tape inside the system. Sadly, those families might have saved themselves enormous frustration if only they had done their research.

We admit it. We didn't do ours as well as we could have. For no other reason than this: we were completely oblivious as to what lay ahead.

Don't let that happen to you.

Here's a real-life example that proves doing your homework might save you in the end. A few years ago, a beloved family friend of ours was sent from a supportive housing facility to the hospital to be treated for cancer. After a few weeks, it became clear that nothing more could be done. Our friend needed long-term care, but no beds were available. She was discharged from the hospital and assigned to a transitional bed in the secure unit of a retirement home. This would be her temporary home as she waited for a more permanent bed at a long-term care facility.

(As you read in the last chapter, *secure unit* is healthcare speak for a unit that is locked to prevent residents who may have dementia or behavioural issues from running off.)

Our friend had the greatest sense of humour you could imagine. Well into her nineties, she was still cracking jokes like Phyllis Diller. But living in a secure unit nearly broke her. Even she couldn't stand being housed in the same ward with people who had dementia and behavioural issues.

With no close family to rely on, she had to advocate on her own behalf to insist on a permanent bed in long-term care. In order to be placed quickly, she was sent to a home that was an hour's drive from her supportive housing community. It was also an hour's drive – or more – from any of her extended family who may have come to visit. That meant she didn't have many visitors. And then, she died. It was heart wrenching.

If only our friend had known she could have put herself on the waiting list for her preferred long-term care home long *before* she became hospitalized, everything might have been different.

Survival Tip:

You can only do so much if you're flying by the seat of your pants. Be proactive.

The Crisis Hits

Preparation will never be more important than during a crisis. Whether your parent is living in the comfort of their own home, a retirement home or supportive housing, they could be in a crisis situation as soon as tomorrow.

That's what happened to our mother. One day she could walk by herself with a walker, the next day she couldn't. A resident can no longer live in supportive housing if they can't walk to the dining room and back. Our mother couldn't do that anymore. We had to move quickly.

It was a situation that came out of left field and hit us like a ton of bricks.

And the same could happen to you.

When it became clear that our mother could no longer walk without assistance, we contacted the LHIN and were assigned a care coordinator.

Mom had been on the LHIN's radar for years, following her cancer treatment a decade or more earlier. She was on file, and staff were aware of her history.

The care coordinator arrived within a day or so to do an assessment.

It was her opinion that our mother was indeed a "crisis case." This meant that she would go on the "crisis list" and be pushed to the head of the line for a long-term care bed. How long would it take before she would receive an offer? There was no way to know for sure.

It took a while for the news to sink in. Mom would need 24-7 assistance from personal support workers and nurses in order to function. On one hand, it made us happy to know that she was going to receive this specialized care. On the other hand, it made us more than a little sad to realize that things would never be the same again.

Now came the truly hard part. Which long-term care homes did we want to include on our list of preferred facilities? Not once had we entertained the thought that Mom would someday need to leave her cozy home in supportive housing. It's embarrassing for us to admit this even now.

We were told that we could list five different facilities. Later, we would discover this to be false – when your parent is on the crisis list, there is no limit to the number of homes you can choose.[12] (More on that in the next chapter.)

You'd think we'd be thrilled to find ourselves at this point in the process.

---

[12] Central LHIN "Choosing a Long-Term Care Home",
     December 31, 2017 http://healthcareathome.ca/central/en/care/
     documents/20171231_ltc_wait_times_public_report_en.pdf

In actual fact, we were terrified. We had no idea which homes to choose, absolutely none. And to make matters worse, we needed to make a decision quickly. Of all the tasks that lay before us, this one was by far the most daunting – daunting because we weren't prepared. We hadn't been proactive in the years leading up to our mom's decline.

Survival Tip:

Ben Franklin knew his stuff. If you fail to plan, you plan to fail.

The Frustration Builds

Our number one frustration? We couldn't understand why our LHIN care coordinator didn't have an information package of some kind that she could give to us, detailing each of the available homes and their features and benefits. It didn't seem like an unreasonable request. We wanted to see photographs and watch videos and read testimonials. We thought surely there must be a centralized storehouse of information that we could consult quickly and efficiently through the LHIN.

We were wrong.

Little did we know that we'd have to play detective and find that information on our own. It was time to put on our rumpled raincoats and play Columbo again.

Our care coordinator did give us a standard form listing all of the homes in our area. It was the first time we had seen the names of the facilities on paper. Some we had heard of, but most we had not. This was the form we would eventually fill out and have our mother sign in order to submit our choices.

The coordinator advised us to go to each home's website for more information. We felt defeated before we'd even begun. There are 86 long-term care facilities in the Hamilton Niagara Haldimand Brant LHIN. Eighty-six. We immediately ruled out those that were too far away from our families and their homes. That still left us with several dozen from which to choose. It was a lot to process. We felt completely overwhelmed.

If and when you find yourself in this position, you'll realize that your parent has likely never seen any of these places. And unless you've visited friends or relatives in long-term care, neither have you. Your assessment can be superficial at best.

But the LHIN made it clear that crisis or no crisis, the onus was on us to schedule tours of these places in order to see them up close and personal before we made our decision. *Schedule tours now? They must be kidding!* we thought. They were not.

We understand now that this research should have been done months or even years earlier. And so, the clock was ticking. We had several days to make a decision. Several days.

Between working and looking after Mom, we were just too exhausted to tour facilities. Instead, we scoured local LTC home websites for photos and videos. Some of the sites were more user-friendly than others. Some seemed designed to encourage tours – not to show a wide array of pictures. This just added to our frustration.

We asked friends for referrals. We searched for reviews online. In the end, after much frustration, we found ourselves relying on the opinion of a trusted relative who works in healthcare. She had had at least some contact with the long-term care homes in our area and gave us her top five picks. Our decision was made. We took a deep breath, said a "Hail Mary" and had our mother sign the paperwork.

Had we done the right thing? We had no idea.

Survival Tip:

We can't emphasize this enough. Start touring long-term care homes in your area now. Begin your research long before you find yourself in a crisis situation. We repeat: *do it now.*

The Waiting Begins

Then came the waiting. It's a bleak process when you stop to think about it. Once you submit your list of choices, you then wait for someone to pass away so that your parent can be offered a bed. This could take weeks. In our mom's case, it took about a month.

Once you receive an offer, you have 24 hours to accept it and five days in which to move. If for any reason you choose to decline the offer, your parent's name must come off the waiting list entirely for three months. Then, they must apply all over again. Those are the rules.

While we waited, we had to figure out how to take care of Mom while she was still in supportive housing. She needed help eating, walking, going to the washroom, getting in and out of bed, and being diapered at night.

For the moment, we had to be her arms and legs. Unfortunately, we weren't trained as PSWs. The work was physically demanding and not for the faint of heart. We weren't sure how long we could last.

Pushing for PSW Care

We needed help. That's when the LHIN suggested we could hire a PSW through a private agency – at our own expense – to give our mother the care that she needed. We called a few agencies and soon realized how expensive this would be. Thirty dollars or more per hour was the norm. A couple of phone calls later, we found a wonderful freelance PSW who was willing to offer a discount if we paid in cash. Even at twenty dollars per hour ($160 for an 8-hour day), it just wasn't sustainable. We began searching for alternatives.

And that's when everything changed.

Our trusted relative, the healthcare worker, told us it was time to get tough. She suggested that too many people simply accept at face value what they're told by their care coordinator. She said in no uncertain terms that we needed to ask for daily PSW care paid for by the government.

We could do this? Really? It simply never occurred to us to question authority on this one. Government budgets being what they are, we figured, "What's the point?"

But our relative insisted that there is money for people who push for it. You just have to push. And so we did. As it turns out, the squeaky wheel got the grease. When we finally pushed the LHIN for PSW care, we were given a surprising number of hours each week. It made all the difference. It helped us to keep our sanity.

And boy, was victory sweet. We basked in the afterglow for days.

That being said, there's no way of knowing for sure whether your parent would be given PSW care in the same situation. But take it from us: You never know until you ask.

Did PSWs cancel at the last minute from time to time? Yes. Did we have to get on the phone each night to confirm that someone was coming the next morning? Yes. Did we have to juggle our schedules when someone cancelled? Absolutely. But for the most part, we did get the help we needed. And we got it because someone "in the know" coached us to push for it.

Survival Tip:

Push. Even if you think the answer might be 'no', ask the question. You've got nothing to lose and everything to gain.

Asking for a New Care Coordinator

Our care coordinator was not the best fit for us. We muddled through as best as we could, believing there was nothing that could be done. We had no idea that, all along, we could have called a supervisor at the LHIN to request a different coordinator.

We found this out from a friend of a friend who was dealing with the LHIN herself on behalf of her elderly mother. She had asked to switch care coordinators in hopes of finding a better fit and was given the okay. According to her, it was a fairly easy process. We were stunned.

One of us was a journalist, and we were still too intimidated to push for what we really wanted.

It's too late for us. But it's not too late for you. If you find yourself in a similar situation, be aware that you have the right to ask for a change.

If you're unhappy with the service you're getting from your care coordinator, you are not stuck with them unless you choose to be. Your tax dollars pay that person's salary. You should receive your money's worth.

Survival Tip:

Speak up if you want a change. You're the customer. Period.

Compiling Your List

"Never put off until tomorrow what you can do today."

—Thomas Jefferson

4

Compiling Your List

"Never put off until tomorrow what you
can do today."

—Thomas Jefferson

Truer words have never been spoken when it comes to arranging long-term care for your parent. Don't put it off. That advice applies if you're in the process of planning your own admission into long-term care, too.

Compiling your list of preferred homes quickly and efficiently is one of the most important things you can do. Take care of it now, and you're in the driver's seat. Arrange tours of the homes you're considering now, talk to the staff and the residents there now, get a feel for each place and make your decision now.

If you choose to put it off, as so many people do, you're in the passenger's seat... and the Ontario long-term care system could very well hijack your mom or dad in a direction they don't want to go. By the time that happens, it's just too late.

Important Info to Keep in Mind

- There are 630 long-term care homes in Ontario: a mixture of municipal, private, not-for-profit and charitable. All of them are regulated by the Ministry of Long-Term Care.[13]
- There are currently 79,000 long-term care beds in Ontario.[14]
- The government has committed to another 15,000 beds within five years, and a further 15,000 in the five years after that.[15]
- According to the Long-Term Care Association of Ontario, an additional 15,000 beds in the system will require nearly 8,500 more full-time care staff than currently exist. That's an increase of 20%.[16]

---

[13] HNHB LHIN Office, March 2019

[14] Long-Term Care Association of Ontario, "This is Long-Term Care", April 2019 https://www.oltca.com/OLTCA/Documents/Reports/TILTC2019web.pdf

[15] Ibid.

[16] Ibid.

Drilling Down to the Details

- If your parent cannot afford around-the-clock in-home care and cannot afford care in a private retirement home like those run by Amica or Seasons, these provincially regulated long-term care homes are their only option.

- Some of the long-term care homes in your LHIN will be lovely. Some may be less than ideal. Your job is to find the ones that your parent would feel comfortable living in and rank them in order from first choice to last.

- You really do need to book tours of the homes in order to see them yourself before you make your decision. According to The Advocacy Centre for the Elderly – a community based legal clinic in Toronto, "you should never apply to a long-term care home you have not seen personally or have not had someone you trust see on your behalf."[17] It's that simple.

- You are permitted to choose as many as five homes if your parent is on the regular waiting list. If your mom or dad is on the crisis list, there is no limit to the number of homes you may choose. We found this out

---

[17] Advocacy Centre for the Elderly, http://www.advocacycentreelderly. org/appimages/file/Long-Term%20Care%20Admission%20Tips%20 and%20Traps%20Stand-Alone.pdf

quite by accident from our care coordinator. She had originally told us we could make up to five selections. A few days later, we asked if we could list five more in order to boost our chances of getting a bed quickly. That's when she informed us we could have done that from the start since our mother was on the crisis list. This was a disappointing bit of miscommunication. Had we listed more homes from the beginning, our mother may have been placed sooner.

- When your parent is on the crisis list, they have priority over others who are simply on the regular waiting list. They are at the head of the line.

- A basic room is equipped with four beds. A semi-private has two beds. A private room has one.

- In many older facilities, residents in a semi-private room share one bathroom that has one entry door. In many newer facilities, residents in a semi-private room share one bathroom that has two entry doors. This could of course make the newer facility more desirable.

- For the most part, it is easier to get a private or semi-private bed. Most basic beds are taken by low income seniors who receive government subsidies to cover the cost.

- Each of the homes charges a standard fee for basic, semi-private and private accommodation. These fees are set by the province.
- Currently in 2019, a basic bed costs $1,891.31 per month, a semi-private bed costs $2,280.04 per month, and a private bed costs $2,701.61 per month.
- Feeling pressure to get a bed quickly? Don't put a home you don't really like on your list – even if it's your last choice. There's every chance you could be offered a bed there. If so, you would have to accept, or come off the list entirely for three months and then start all over again.

Your care coordinator will give you a printed list of the homes in your area. You will check off the boxes beside those homes that you want on your list, number your choices, and then check one, two or all three of the boxes that indicate basic, semi-private or private beds.

If your parent is a crisis case and you are desperate for a bed in long-term care, checking off all three bed options is a strategy that would likely give you a better chance of a quick offer. You are not obliged to do this, however.

Be aware that there is a drawback to using the above strategy. For example: Your parent is a crisis case and wants a private bed. You select all three bed options for the sake of getting into long-term care quickly, believing that you will be able to transfer to a private bed at some point soon. Your parent is offered a semi-private bed and accepts it. They are taken off the crisis list. They have been placed. They are no longer a crisis case because they are now receiving care. Someone who is still a crisis case may take precedence over your parent for any private bed that may open up in that facility. As a result, your mom or dad may accept a semi-private bed or a basic bed – thinking a private bed is a real possibility. In reality, they may stay in that semi-private or basic bed much longer than they imagined they would. Potentially for years.

If your experience is anything like ours, you may be told that if you don't get the first choice of the homes on your list, you can accept the bed you are offered – wherever it may be – and remain on the regular waiting list for your first choice. You may get the impression that this will be a simple process, and that you will be able to move your parent to their top pick fairly easily and quickly. If this happens to you, you have been misinformed. We were later told by an independent source that this process could actually take a number of years. It is not fast. It is not a given. Do not count on it happening.

If your parent is not a crisis case and time is not of the essence, they may be willing to wait for admission to the one and only home they really want. Just be aware that someone who is a crisis case may be offered a bed there before your parent is.

Remember that distance is an issue. No matter how good a home's reputation, think twice before you add it to your list if it's a long drive from where you live. If you plan to visit your parent daily, a 2-hour car ride each day – or longer – grows tiring quickly.

Remember that you can access a complete list of the homes in your area online. We had no idea this was possible. Remember, too, that you can also access a profile page for each home that includes bed waiting times and inspection reports.

Still with us? Good. It's a lot of information to take in, we know. At the end of the day, it's everything we can think of that might help you and your family make it through the process of compiling your list of homes with greater ease than we did.

Survival Tip:

Thomas Jefferson was right: "Never put off until tomorrow what you can do today." Start compiling your list now.

Waiting for an Offer

"I say patience, and shuffle the cards."

—Miguel de Cervantes,
Don Quixote

5

Waiting for an Offer

"I say patience, and shuffle the cards."

—Miguel de Cervantes,
Don Quixote

Patience is the name of the game when you're waiting for a long-term care bed. If patience isn't your strong suit now, you'd better start cultivating it. Once we submitted our list of preferred facilities, we waited. We had no idea how long it would take before a bed might become available. Every morning, we woke up wondering if today would be the day the phone would ring. It was more than a little nerve wracking.

We also knew the rules. Whenever a bed was offered, we would have 24 hours to decide whether or not to accept it. If we accepted, we would have five days in which to pack up our mother's supportive housing suite and move her to long-term care. If we chose to decline the offer *for any reason*, her name would come off the waiting list for three months, and we would have to submit our choices all over again.

Why would someone decline a bed? Perhaps because they've reconsidered applying for a basic bed and now want to go the semi-private or private route. That's one potential scenario. There are as many reasons as there are people.

Our family had an interesting reason for declining a bed – one that you might learn from. After a couple of weeks on the crisis list, our mother was offered a bed in a facility that was indeed on our list, but was not our first, second or even third choice. We had no option but to accept it. Fortunately, the home was in "flu outbreak" mode when the offer was made, so we didn't have to move right away. We would have to wait until the outbreak order was lifted.

We had no idea how lucky we were.

A visit to the facility to check it out revealed that residents could only bring "wipeable furniture" into their room… chairs covered in vinyl, leather, or plastic. The policy was in place for reasons of health and hygiene, but our LHIN caseworker neglected to tell us that some homes had these types of policies. We were completely blindsided.

We had recently bought our mom an expensive lift chair that happened to be upholstered in plush fabric. Lift chairs raise and lower electronically to make sitting down and getting up easier. Mom adored hers. It was one of the few things in life that still brought her pleasure and a feeling of safety and security. Leaving it behind was not an option. We were certain that if we took the chair away from her, she would simply give up.

Thanks to the chair issue, the LHIN allowed us to cancel our acceptance of the first offer. That meant that Mom was back on the crisis list. About a week later, a new offer for a private bed was extended to us, and we accepted. It was one of our top five choices and was reasonably close geographically to everyone in our family. To say that it was a relief is an understatement. We felt as if a real weight had been lifted. You probably will, too.

Survival Tip:

If your parent has a favourite upholstered chair, consult with your care coordinator to find out which of the homes on your list have a "wipeable furniture policy" and which do not.

More Details

Offer accepted, it was time to consider more details. "How big would our mom's room be?" was the first one. "Would there be room for her lift chair?" was the second. Because we had never toured the home that she'd be living in, we had no information to work with at all. Measurements weren't available on the home's website, so we were flying blind… again.

Happily, a quick visit to the home was all that was needed to confirm the measurements. Our concern was that there would be enough room beside the hospital bed and bedside table for Mom's lift chair. And there was. Just. Somebody up there was looking down on us.

Survival Tip:

Don't leave it to chance the way we did. Take tours and take room measurements at the homes on your list. Write the information down in your dedicated notebook or key it into the Notes app on your smartphone. You may not think so now, but this information will be invaluable to you down the road.

Amenities

We may not have toured the homes on our list, but we did make contact with them by phone to inquire about the amenities provided. We knew that Mom's new home would offer a modest room with limited space for private furnishings. She would have a hospital bed, a bedside table with drawers, a small built-in closet and a unit of some kind that would be big enough for a television and storage space, and a window. Her 2-piece bathroom would be wheelchair accessible, with plenty of room for her to sit in front of the sink to brush her teeth or hair if she was able. The toilet would have a raised seat, and there would be dispensers on the wall for hand soap, baby wipes and plastic gloves for the PSWs.

Long-term care would provide nursing care 24 hours a day, 7 days a week. It would also provide control and administration of all medication, a twice weekly shower, laundry service, and assistance from personal support workers for getting out of bed, toileting, dressing, wheeling to the dining room and back, feeding if necessary, and getting into bed after meals and at night.

It was a little piece of paradise.

On move-in day, it all became real. The room felt small, but it was efficient. It had everything Mom would need within arm's reach, and that's what mattered.

The wait for a bed was over. Our journey, of course, was not.

Know Where to Look for Answers Online

"It is easy to discover what another has discovered before."

-Christopher Columbus

6

Know Where to Look for Answers Online

"It is easy to discover what another has discovered before."

-Christopher Columbus

We talked about asking great questions a few chapters ago.

But what if you don't get the answers you're looking for? Time and again, the bureaucrats we dealt with suggested it wasn't their job to help us with the details. Not only did we find that hard to believe, we found it unacceptable.

Like it or not, there'll be times when you'll need to look for answers to your questions online – just like we did. You may not consider yourself to be all that tech savvy. Guess what? The internet is about to become your new best friend. *You just need to know where to look.*

Our job is to show you the way.

It was our experience that the LHIN and the Ministry of Health and Ministry of Long-Term Care websites are simply not user-friendly. At all. Trying to find meaningful information without someone guiding you is like trying to find a proverbial needle in a haystack. It's buried… buried so deeply under layers and layers of tabs and links and alphabets that only a bureaucrat would know how to find their way. Think we're exaggerating? We are not.

The thought occurred to us that our tax dollars are funding the creation of these government websites. We're the customer. And no customer should ever have to go down a rabbit hole looking for help. That help should be easy to access and simple to understand. Period.

In a way, we feel a bit like Christopher Columbus… explorers at heart. He discovered the new world; we discovered the resources you need inside these complex websites. He sailed the ocean; we surfed the internet.

Ready to hang ten? Let's do this.

Question #1: What LHIN am I in?

Each of the 14 LHINs has its own individual website. Before you do anything, you need to know which

LHIN covers your area so that you can find information specific to your family.

Look here:

1. Go to: **http://www.lhins.on.ca/**
2. Enter your postal code in the search window
3. Click on the **Find** button.

A link to the LHIN website for your area will pop up on the screen.

Question #2: Which long-term care facilities are located in my LHIN?

Now that you know the name of your LHIN, you'll need to find the complete list of long-term care facilities in your area. What follows is the easiest way for you to access it. We won't even tell you how many steps we had to go through in order to find this web page. You wouldn't believe us if we did.

Look here:

1. Go to: **http://www.health.gov.on.ca/en/ public/programs/ltc/home-finder.aspx**
2. You'll notice a search window with two dropdown menus below it at bottom of the page. Go to the second dropdown menu entitled **Select a LHIN**

3. Select the name of your region's LHIN.

Shazam! – the list will appear.

Question #3: Where can I find information about each home?

It's simple.

Look here:

Notice that the names of each home on the list you just found appear in blue.

1. Click on the name of the facility you're interested in, and you'll be taken to a profile page.

    Look at the left side of the page. You will see the name, address and email address of the home as well as links to home inspection reports, links to average wait times for a bed, the number of licensed beds, and the name of the administrator of the home.

2. Click on **Home's Inspection Reports** under the heading **Home Links**. This will take you to the most recent inspections by the Ministry of Long-Term Care.

3. Click on the **Home Profile** tab beside the **Inspections** tab at the top of the page for basic information about the facility.

4. Take a look at the top right corner of the home profile page. You will see the heading **Inspection Information**, which will tell you whether or not improvement is required, as well as how many non-compliance orders the home has received compared to the provincial average.

When we stumbled onto this info as part of our research, our jaws dropped to the floor. We didn't know that profile pages for each home existed when we were compiling our list of desired homes. We had no idea that you could see each facility's inspection information online. At no time did our LHIN care coordinator show us this site, nor did she explain how we could find it for ourselves.

Question #4: What "placement priority category" does my mom or dad fall into?

In true bureaucratic style, the LHIN has what it calls placement priority categories. Your parent will be assessed and then assigned to one of these categories. Whichever one they are assigned to will have a bearing on the speed with which they may be offered a bed.

Look here:

Check out the categories on the final page of this document:

http://healthcareathome.ca/hnhb/en/care/
Documents/Long-term%20care%20wait%20
time%20reporting%20Jul%202019%20-%20
Hamilton%20En.pdf

[or https://bit.ly/2lTwLn1]

Trying to figure out your parent's odds of quick placement according to this document is pretty much an impossible task. But looking at it will at least help you to understand some of the factors at play when it comes to where your mom or dad is slotted on the waiting list.

Question #5: What are the current wait times for a bed in the homes I've chosen?

Before you submit your list of choices, check the wait times for a bed in each facility. This will give you at least some idea of your chances of receiving an offer soon. Again, we had no idea that this information was available online.

Look here:

There are two ways to do this. Here's the first.

1. Follow the link below to the master list of homes in your LHIN.

http://www.health.gov.on.ca/en/public/ programs/ltc/home-finder.aspx

2. Select your LHIN in the dropdown menu.
3. Click on the home you'd like to check, and you'll be taken to the profile page.
4. On the left side of the page, under **Home Details**, you'll see a link that reads **Average Wait Times**. Click on that link, click on your LHIN, click on your town or city, and you'll go to a PDF document featuring a chart.

Here's another method that is somewhat more direct.

1. Click on the link below and scroll to the bottom of the page.

https://hssontario.ca/important-links/ long-term-care-wait-times-and-waitlists

2. Click on your LHIN then click on your desired location at the bottom of that page, and you're in.

3. Scroll down for the chart – you will see the average number of beds that become available each month on the far right.

You'll notice, the chart also shows the number of licensed beds in the home, the number of people on the waitlist for basic, semi-private and private beds, and the number of days – statistically – that 9 out of 10 people have waited for an offer.

Again, we didn't know that this existed.

Question #6 Where can I see complaints that have been registered?

We suggest that you research any complaints that may have been registered against the homes you're interested in.

Look here:

1. Go to: **http://publicreporting.ltchomes.net/ en-ca/Default.aspx**
2. Click on **Find home by name** and select the home you're interested in.
3. Click on the **Inspections** tab. The complaints inspections are listed in blue. Click on each one, and you'll be able to read a Ministry report.

Again, we had no idea that this set-up existed. We found out about it after the fact from a friend of ours who is a Health Inspector in Ontario. She knows the system. Unfortunately, not everyone has a friend on the inside who can offer meaningful advice.

Question #7: How do I complain about my parent's facility?

As a customer of the long-term care system, you have every right to bring your concerns to the attention of the people in charge.

Look here:

Each home is required by law to inform every resident on how to make a complaint and must post the information in a public place inside the facility.

Residents and their families can make a complaint to a staff member, the licensee of the home, or the Residents' Council at the home. The licensee must investigate and resolve the issue where possible within ten business days of receiving the complaint. Where this isn't possible, they must acknowledge the complaint and offer a date by which a resolution may be reached.

But that's not the only way to lodge a complaint.

Look here:

There is also a government hotline that you can call. (Again, we had no idea that this existed.)

You can lodge a complaint about alleged abuse, resident care, medical care, resident rights, financial concerns, dietary concerns, or concerns about the administration or the physical environment of the home.

Call the toll-free **Long-Term Care ACTION Line**. It's open seven days a week from 8:30 a.m. to 7:00 p.m. EST at 1-866-434-0144.

You're not required to give your name and address, but common sense dictates you'll have a better chance of seeing the issue resolved if you do.

Note: If you have already contacted the home directly and have called the ACTION LINE with no resolution, there is a last resort. Call the Patient Ombudsman toll-free at 1-888-321-0339.

Question #8: How do I complain about my LHIN?

Yes, you really can lodge a complaint about your LHIN.

Look here:

Just call the **Long-Term Care ACTION LINE**: 1-866-434-0144. Ask to be connected with an Independent

Complaints Facilitator (ICF). Think of them as a liaison who will take your concerns seriously.

According to the Ministry of Health and the Ministry of Long-Term Care websites, the ICF will return your call within ten business days.[18]

Question #9: How can I be better informed about the long-term care industry?

Check out this comprehensive PDF report from the Ontario Long-Term Care Association. We can't recommend it highly enough.

Look here:

1. Go to **https://oltca.com/OLTCA/**
2. Scroll down to **"This is Long-Term Care 2019"** **report available now**.
3. Click on **Read it here** at the bottom of the paragraph.

This association is the largest of its kind in Canada and the only one that represents what it calls "the full mix of long-term care operators: private, not-for-profit, charitable and municipal."

---

[18] Ministry of Health, Ministry of Long-Term Care, 2019 http://www. health.gov.on.ca/en/common/system/services/lhin/ltc_actionline.aspx

The report is loaded with useful information. It doesn't pull any punches, either. Among other things, it highlights the serious need for more staff in long-term care homes, thanks to the growing demographic of seniors who require care.

Question #10: Can I get financial aid if I take a leave of absence from my job to help care for my parent?

This may be a very important issue for you and your family. When our mother's health began to decline, one of us was still working, the other was retired. Until we had a conversation with a union rep, we had no idea that a federal government program called Employment Insurance Compassionate Care Benefits existed.

The government website states:

> Through Employment Insurance, you could receive financial assistance of up to 55% of your earnings, to a maximum of $562 a week. These benefits will help you take time away from work to provide care or support to a critically ill or injured person or someone needing end-of-life care.[19]

What a revelation.

---

[19] Government of Canada, Benefits for Caregivers, 2019 https://www.canada.ca/en/services/benefits/ei/caregiving.html

The thing is, the general public doesn't seem to know much about it. Had we not called a union rep, we might have been in the dark for months, not realizing that EI could have taken some of the financial burden off of our shoulders.

The process was fairly simple. We had to ask our mother's doctor to certify that Mom had a serious medical condition with a significant risk of death within 26 weeks. Once this was done, the document was processed, and EI topped up the reduced salary in question so that no money was lost.

Look here:

Here's a link to the Government of Canada website that explains the program. (In our view, the explanation is somewhat confusing.)

https://www.canada.ca/en/financial-consumer-agency/services/caring-someone-ill/benefits-tax-credits-caregivers.html

[or https://bit.ly/31W5f8w]

There's no doubt that you'll have questions. The bottom line is this: either you're eligible for the program or you're not. We recommend that you speak to your employer's human resources department and call your local MP's office for clarification as well. We found the staff in our MP's constituency office to be extremely kind, compassionate and helpful. Much to our delight, they cared.

Need some help finding your MP's contact number? Go to the Elections Canada website:

https://www.elections.ca/scripts/vis/FindED?L=e&PAGEID=20

…then enter your postal code beside the **Search** button.

You'll find your Member of Parliament's name on the right side of the page, along with a link to their contact info.

A word to the wise. Take as many notes as you can during the conversations you have about this program. It is quite confusing. Don't hang up the phone until you understand all of the details, as well as what your next steps are. And don't be afraid to call your MP's office multiple times if you have more questions.

Survival Tip:

Columbus used the North Star to navigate his way to the new world. Think of this chapter as your North Star. Follow the instructions here, and they'll lead you to the online answers you and your family truly need.

Life in Long-Term Care

"All God's angels come to us disguised."

—James Russell Lowell

7

Life in Long-Term Care

"All God's angels come to us disguised."

—James Russell Lowell

For all the moments of frustration you'll experience on this journey, you will also find moments of peace, joy and contentment… all thanks to the loving angels you'll meet along the way.

The PSWs who were assigned to our mom in long-term care were the most kind-hearted, compassionate souls imaginable. They greeted her with a cheery "Good morning, Verna!" at 6 a.m., washed her, toileted her, helped put her teeth in, dressed her, and wheeled her to the dining room and back again after each meal. They repositioned her in bed when she became uncomfortable and brought her snacks and fresh water all day long. They were love personified. The nurses were, too – always ready to administer additional medication whenever Mom's pain became unbearable.

It won't take long for you to notice, however, the degree to which these angels are overworked, exhausted and slowly burning out.

Understaffing

In January of 2019, CBC's *Marketplace* broadcast an episode that saw a producer go undercover with a hidden camera inside a Toronto-area long-term care home. Much of what CBC encountered there, we saw with our own eyes in our mom's facility. Don't get us wrong. Our mother's long-term care home was lovely. Be that as it may, there seem to be issues common to both good places and bad ones.

Understaffing, for one, is a real concern. The call bells that residents pushed for help at our mom's facility would often ring for extended periods of time. There weren't enough staff available to answer them all in a timely way. When PSWs or nurses called in sick, they couldn't always be replaced on short notice. From the outside looking in, we found this shocking. We soon discovered that all of this is considered normal by those on the inside.

On our mother's ward, just two PSWs worked the early morning shift. They had the task of waking up more than a dozen residents, getting them washed and dressed, wheeling them to the dining room, then preparing and serving the food. They also had to feed those patients who were no longer able to feed themselves. After the meal, they would wheel everyone back to their rooms and get ready to start all over again in preparation for lunch. It was a real marathon.

The nurses were swamped, too. The RN on duty each shift at our mother's home was so overloaded with work that we got into the habit of prefacing our request for more medication for Mom with the words, "We know you're busy, but when you have a chance, could you please help us?"

Each evening, we would call our mother to ask how she was feeling. It was common for her to tell us that she was still in her wheelchair – an hour after dinner had finished – and was still waiting for a PSW to take her to the washroom.

It was awful to hear her tell this story night after night. But that wasn't the worst of it. We would calmly do our best to reassure Mom that someone would be there soon, all the while knowing that that probably wasn't the truth. We'd hang up the phone and call the nurse's station to ask for help. Sometimes the phone would go unanswered. Why? Because the nurse was too busy elsewhere… nursing.

In the end, there's one thing we know for sure: the PSWs and nurses in long-term care facilities have the very best of intentions. *There just aren't enough of them.* A petition is now circulating in many homes in Ontario in support of something known as Bill 13, the *Time to Care Act.* It's proposed legislation that would require long-term care homes in Ontario to provide "a minimum care standard of an average of four hours of hands-on care to residents each day." Will it become law? Stay tuned.

In the meantime, there is a human tsunami heading our way. It's a tidal wave of mothers and fathers who will soon need a higher level of care than they currently enjoy in their own homes, their retirement homes, or supportive housing facilities.

In our view, the current system just isn't up to the task.[20]

Survival Tip:

Be prepared to see caregivers in your mom or dad's facility being overworked. Try to show them compassion, love and appreciation whenever you can.

---

[20] A version of the opening to this chapter first appeared as an opinion piece in the *Hamilton Spectator*. May 10, 2019. https://www.thespec. com/opinion-story/9347596-our-mom-s-long-term-care-journey-was-a-long-and-winding-road-that-was-exhausting-at-every-turn/

Noise and Behaviour

Overworked caregivers aren't the only issue you'll run into in long-term care. Noise and behavioural issues are two more. Some of the residents in our mother's facility suffered from dementia; they moaned and screamed for what sometimes felt like forever. Some lay their heads down on the dining room table at mealtimes; some took a doll with them everywhere they went. Most of these patients were unable to speak. This really bothered our mother when she first arrived. She felt she had no one to talk with at mealtimes, and she was right.

The only woman seated at Mom's table who did not suffer from dementia passed away within weeks of our mother's arrival. That was a rough day. It may sound like a small thing, but in reality, it was a big one. Having come from a supportive housing facility where there was lots of social interaction, our mother was expecting that to continue in long-term care. Unfortunately, it wasn't possible.

Survival Tip:

If your mom or dad is still of sound mind, prepare them in advance for this sad reality: they may not be able to have conversations with other residents during their meals.

Dementia

Fortunately for us, both our mother and father were of sound mind until the end. Many of our friends have not been so lucky. One friend whose mother lived with Alzheimer's had a particularly tough experience. She chose to hire around-the-clock PSWs so that her mom could stay in her own home in familiar surroundings. Unfortunately, there were multiple issues with caregivers calling in sick and/or quitting on the spur of the moment. It was a stressful time for the whole family.

Not everyone chooses to arrange in-home care for a parent with dementia. If you're looking for a long-term care facility for your mom or dad, the Alzheimer Society of Ontario has an excellent list of tips for you. Click on the link below to learn more about choosing the right facility for your parent:

https://alzheimer.ca/en/on/Living-with-dementia/
Caring-for-someone/Long-term-care/Finding-
a-home

[or https://bit.ly/2AJhfOI]

The Society also has a fabulous checklist designed to arm you with great questions before you tour the long-term care facilities on your list. Click on the link below to print the PDF for future reference:

https://alzheimer.ca/sites/default/files/files/national/long-term-care/ltc_1_care_home_checklist_e.pdf

[or https://bit.ly/355AFLZ]

Elder Abuse and Violence

Elder abuse and violence among residents are serious concerns in long-term care homes of course, too. The Ontario Health Coalition is a watchdog for the province's public healthcare system. In January of 2019, its "Situation Critical" report stated that there were at least 27 homicides in Ontario's long-term care homes in the five years leading up to the report. All of them were as a result of resident-on-resident violence.[21] Experts say this violence usually involves at least one patient with dementia, which, they add, can manifest as aggression.[22] Violence against long-term care staff – PSWs and nurses – is common as well.[23]

---

[21] CBC.ca January 20, 2019 https://www.cbc.ca/news/health/long-term-care-residents-violence-deaths-killed-1.4985946
The Ontario Health Coalition http://www.ontariohealthcoalition.ca/wp-content/uploads/FINAL-LTC-REPORT.pdf

[22] Ibid.

[23] The Ontario Health Coalition http://www.ontariohealthcoalition.ca/wp-content/uploads/FINAL-LTC-REPORT.pdf

We feel fortunate that we saw absolutely no evidence of abuse or violence where our mother lived. That being said, every home is different, and every group of residents is different.

If you should encounter these issues in your parent's facility, bring them to the attention of the home's director of care immediately. If the situation isn't resolved to your satisfaction, remember that you can call the Long-Term Care ACTION Line at 1-866-434-0144 to lodge a complaint.

Survival Tip:

Do your homework long before your parent ever moves into long-term care. As part of your research, check the home inspection reports online for complaints about resident-on-resident violence.

Project Managing

Life in long-term care is a new adventure every day. Whatever the issue may be inside your parent's facility, get used to taking action. Adopt the mindset that you are project managing your parent's care.

In our case, we encountered daily confusion: phone calls weren't always returned, healthcare professionals weren't always available to give us updates, next steps weren't always clearly explained. "I'm sorry, I don't understand," became our new favourite phrase. We questioned things again and again, looking for simple answers to help us move forward.

Communication

Above all, we couldn't understand why the different professionals assigned to our mother didn't seem to communicate with each other regularly. The day shift nurse didn't always read the notes on the computer file that were made by the overnight nurse. The physiotherapist didn't report his findings to our mother's doctor. The occupational therapist didn't discuss new developments with Mom's nurse. It just didn't make sense to us.

We walked around with quizzical expressions on our faces as we tried to untangle each day's events. Our brains literally hurt. We thought we were savvy women, but much of the time, we didn't feel savvy at all.

Palliative Care

Seven months before Mom went into long-term care, she spent several weeks in the hospital. The ER doctor referred her to a palliative care doctor, who was a lovely woman. This doc came to Mom's bedside one morning and had a truly beautiful conversation with her about death.

The words "palliative care" initially filled us with dread. To us, they meant *your mother is dying right now*. The doctor took time to educate us.

"What *palliative* really means," she told us, "is that your mother is coming to the end of her life."

These words came as a huge comfort. No one was dying just yet. It would be some time before that was to come.

Mom was assigned a palliative care team composed of this doctor and a nurse. They came to visit our mother in her supportive housing suite several times before she moved to long-term care. Their job was to check on her status and determine whether her health was stable or on the decline.

At one point, we asked our mother's family doctor whether Mom might be admitted to a hospice. We had no idea what the criteria was. It was then we were told that palliative care can be given just as effectively in long-term care as it can in a hospice setting. That came as a relief. There are other factors at play, of course, when it comes to being admitted to a hospice. For us, the advantage of remaining in long-term care was that it avoided another move and more upheaval for our mom.

If you're looking for information online about palliative care for seniors, here's a heads-up: it isn't as easy to find as you might think. Check out this link to the Ministry of Health and the Ministry of Long-Term Care websites for some basic details:

http://www.health.gov.on.ca/en/public/programs/palliative/palliative_questionsandanswers.aspx

Survival Tip:

Life in long-term care will be different every day. Some of it good, some not so good. Breathe, smile, go with the flow, and before you know it, you'll be project managing your mom or dad's care like a pro.

Shopping for Mom or Dad

"The closest thing to being cared for is to care for someone else."

—Carson McCullers

8

Shopping for Mom or Dad

"The closest thing to being cared for is to care for someone else."

—Carson McCullers

Anyone who has ever been a caregiver knows that there is much more to the job than meets the eye. You are chief cook and bottle washer – and then some. That means you'll find yourself at the local big box store on a fairly regular basis. The good news is that you won't need to shop for much of anything when your mom or dad moves to long-term care. All of their needs will be looked after. But when they're still at home or in supportive housing waiting for an LTC bed, you'll probably be at the store quite often.

Incontinence Products

If your parent is incontinent, you'll likely be buying a large number of adult briefs, diapers and/or pads. Tena, Depends, and Poise are three of the leading brands.

When our mother was in supportive housing and no longer able to walk, she switched from adult briefs to the taped variety designed like a child's diaper. We found these much easier to put on and take off of her while she was lying down in bed. (Learning this technique, by the way, was a bigger challenge than you might imagine. Ask a PSW to teach you how to do it properly.)

Sad to say, there is no provincial government assistance or subsidy for the purchase of incontinence products. If your parent is registered with Veterans Affairs Canada, however, they may be able to apply for financial assistance. Click on the link below or call VAC toll-free: 1-866-522-2122.

https://www.veterans.gc.ca/eng/health-support

Survival Tip:

It's surprising how quickly the cost of incontinence products adds up. We recommend buying in bulk. Watch the sales at Walmart, Costco, and your local drugstore, and buy a 2 or 3 month supply each time you go shopping.

Compression Socks

If your mom or dad suffers from edema – swollen legs or feet – you may have to buy compression socks. Your parent's family doctor must write a prescription, which you will then fill at a drugstore that sells mobility aids.

Compression socks are sized according to the amount of pressure or compression they offer. Ready for your science lesson today?

8–15 mmHg offers the lightest form of compression. (mmHg stands for *millimetres of mercury* – a measurement of pressure.)

The sizing scale gradually increases to 30–40 mmHg, which is often prescribed for severe edema and varicose veins. 40–50 mmHg offers the highest level of compression.

If you have to go down this road, you'll soon discover that compression socks are quite challenging to get on and off. Your parent's nurse and/or PSWs will be assigned this task.

Survival Tip:

Be extra sure that you understand the exact size of sock you should be buying. Verify the size with your parent's doctor before you make the purchase. Compression socks can be fairly expensive, and once put on, usually can't be returned.

Medication

While Mom was still in her supportive housing suite, a nurse acquaintance of ours convinced us to order her medication from the drugstore in a blister pack. Up to that point, Mom's pills had been dispensed in bottles. Once a week, she sorted the pills herself and put them in a 7-day pill box.

We were amazed at how much easier the blister pack made life for us.

It was delivered once a week, with pills in separate plastic sections for breakfast, lunch, dinner and bedtime. We found the pack to be extremely convenient. You might, too.

First, though, a word to the wise. Several times, the drugstore didn't assemble Mom's blister pack correctly. Nighttime pills were mixed up with daytime pills, which could have been dangerous.

Don't let this happen to you.

Survival Tip:

Be sure to take a photo of the top row of the blister pack, showing the correct pills for breakfast, lunch, dinner and bedtime.

Whenever a new pack arrives from the pharmacy, check to make sure that each row is identical to the photo.

On the bright side, once your mom or dad is in long-term care, their medication will be sourced, dispensed and administered 24-7 by the nurse on duty. No more calls to the drugstore. We found it a real relief to have someone else take over. You probably will, too.

Mobile Blood Work

Granted, blood work isn't something that you shop for. Nevertheless, you may need to shop for a blood work provider who can make house calls.

Most long-term care homes only have a specialized healthcare provider on site once a week to do blood work. Unfortunately, there may be times when your mom or dad is in an emergency situation and needs to have it done right away.

That was our mom's story. When she became ill one Sunday, her nurse recommended immediate blood work. Because it was a weekend, we had no choice but to take Mom by ambulance to the local hospital, which we did. Had we been able to wait until Monday, we could have called LifeLabs. It has mobile units that make house calls in locations across Ontario. LifeLabs charges $60 for a home visit. They also do other tests in addition to blood work. Check out the link below, scroll down to the middle of the page and click on **Request my Home Appointment** under the heading **My Visit**:

https://www.lifelabs.com/tests-services/mobile-lab-services/

Survival Tip:

There are healthcare companies out there whose mission it is to make your life easier. Take the time now to educate yourself about the services they provide. You'll thank yourself down the road.

Buying Adaptive Clothing

"The art of life lies in a constant readjustment to our surroundings."

—Okakura Kakuzō

9

Buying Adaptive Clothing

"The art of life lies in a constant
readjustment to our surroundings."

—Okakura Kakuzō

Something that may catch you off guard when you're
least expecting it is your mom or dad's need for adaptive
clothing. As their mobility decreases, they may need
clothes, shoes, and other products designed to help
them function with greater ease.

Now more than ever, they need to adapt. The right
clothing for your mom or dad may prevent a fall or
injury. Providing them with well-made products is a
must.

Take our mom for example. She suffered from
congestive heart failure, kidney issues and edema. Her
feet were incredibly swollen. Edema happens when
your small blood vessels leak fluid into your tissues.

While she was still able to walk, Mom needed rubber soled slippers that would accommodate her swollen feet.

Thanks to a tip from one of her PSWs, we found a national company out of Toronto called Silvert's Adaptive Clothing & Footwear and called for a catalogue. What a godsend. Among other things, Silvert's sells slippers that use a Velcro closure on top of the foot. Without them, our mom wouldn't have been able to walk safely.

(You'll find a full listing of Canadian companies that sell adaptive products in the second half of this chapter.)

Whichever company you order from, we suggest calling directly to speak to a customer representative before ordering a slipper or shoe. Initially, we ordered a size that was too small, and we had to send the box back. The service rep was really helpful and gave us precise instructions on how to measure for the right fit. (You need to measure while your mom or dad is standing up.)

Meanwhile, our mother's PSWs also told us about something called a "hospital sock," which has rubber traction on the sole. These socks were a lifesaver. Mom could keep them on in bed at night. If she had to get up to use the bathroom, the PSWs didn't have to put slippers on her feet; she could simply walk to the bathroom, secure in the knowledge that her socks were non-slip.

We also ordered a special wheelchair blanket that was great for winter weather. Soft and washable, it featured Velcro straps that wrapped around the armrests of Mom's wheelchair. She loved it.

Booming Industry

Months later, it makes us smile to remember what newbies we were. We had no idea how big the adaptive clothing industry is.

These products are invaluable for so many different kinds of people.

For example, stroke victims who can no longer put their arms into sleeves or their legs into pants. They're also useful for people confined to wheelchairs who need coats that wrap around both their body and the chair. Special clothing exists, too, for people with Alzheimer's who need simple Velcro closures instead of buttons. You'll find a wide range of products for people who are incontinent, too. And that's just the tip of the iceberg.

So imagine our surprise when we discovered that there is actually an **Adaptive Clothing** page on selected

LHIN websites – a page that could have educated us about these products. Sadly, we didn't find out about it until we were in the midst of doing the research for this book. Again, an unfortunate failure to communicate on the part of someone – we're not sure who – inside the system.

To find the adaptive clothing page for your LHIN, Google the name of your LHIN along with "healthline. ca" and "adaptive clothing" in the same search window. You should be able to find the correct page easily. Notice the coloured tabs at the top of the page. This is where you select your specific town or city. In some cases, there simply is no adaptive clothing category listed.

Can you imagine trying to find this page on your own without knowing the correct search terms? And trying to find it using the LHIN home page as your starting point would be just as confusing. We had to ask a receptionist at our local Hamilton Niagara Haldimand Brant LHIN to walk us through the process.

Again, the thought occurred to us that our tax dollars paid for someone to create these website pages. Sadly, the pages themselves are often buried so deeply inside the mother ship that you'd be hard pressed to ever find them on your own.

We've said it before and we'll say it again. Not only do we find this hard to believe, we find it unacceptable. People need information that is user-friendly and easily accessible. Period.

For demonstration purposes now, here is a link to the adaptive clothing page on the Hamilton Niagara Haldimand Brant LHIN site:

https://www.hnhbhealthline.ca/listServices. aspx?id=10626&region=HNHB

Remember, adaptive clothing retailers are experts. Many have been in business for years, so don't hesitate to contact them to ask for their advice. We used Silvert's for all of our purchases; we didn't know that other companies existed. Check out this list of stores that ship across Canada:

Silvert's Adaptive Clothing & Footwear can be reached toll-free at 1-800-387-7088, or online:

http://www.silverts.com/?adv=IDG

Monarch Clothes in Waterloo is a stylish option:

https://monarchclothes.com/

Down-Under Wool in Niagara Falls specializes in bed-sore prevention and treatment. Its products are made from medical grade sheepskin and merino wool from Australia:

https://www.medicalsheepskins.com/

Toronto's **Adapted Clothing on the Net** can be reached at:

https://www.adaptedclothing-onthenet.com/

Geri Fashions is located in Oakville:

https://www.gerifashions.com/

EasyWear Adaptive Clothing is headquartered in Cambridge:

https://www.easywearadaptiveclothing.com/

Survival Tip:

Help is out there. Spread the word to friends and family that these adaptive clothing stores exist. You'll be thrilled at the difference their products will make to your mom or dad.

Special Clothing for Eating

Eating presents its own challenges in long-term care. As your parent continues to decline, they'll be more likely to need a bib during meals to protect their clothing from spills and stains. The bibs provided by the homes are definitely adequate, but often look a little tired and institutional.

We found it kind of sad to look around the dining room and see the residents wearing the same blue plaid day after day.

So, we got busy at the sewing machine and created some pretty bibs – the kind that crafty types call dining scarves. We knew that if they had an elegant name, our mother would be more likely to agree to wear them. To our delight, it worked. We shopped for bright, cheery fabrics and whipped up a series of bibs that attached at the base of the neck with Velcro closures. Happily, they lifted the spirits of everyone concerned – residents and caregivers alike. It became a pleasure to look across the table at our mom when she was wearing bright, cheerful colours near her face. Life affirming, you know?

If you sew, it's simple to draft a pattern. Just borrow a bib from your parent's long-term care home and trace it. If you'd rather buy one ready-made, you'll find them online at some of the adaptive clothing companies listed above.

Looking for something on the elegant side? Lots of entrepreneurs make and sell their own version of dining scarves online. Picture a long scarf that hangs around the neck and lays flat down the front of a blouse or shirt. Take a look at this link on Etsy:

https://www.etsy.com/ca/search?q=dining%20 scarves%20for%20elderly

Making mealtimes a little more cheerful is a small thing that makes a big difference in long-term care. Get your creative groove on and have some fun with it!

Survival Tip:

It's tempting to stress out over all of this. There's really no need. The more you research these clothing providers, the more you'll enjoy the thrill of finding just the right product to make life more comfortable for your mom or dad.

Buying and Renting
Assistive Devices

"We rise by lifting others."

—Robert Ingersoll

10

Buying and Renting Assistive Devices

"We rise by lifting others."

—Robert Ingersoll

We all need someone to lift our spirits from time to time. Your elderly mom or dad may need more than that; they could require a special piece of furniture to lift them physically.

Many elderly people have a beloved chair that they spend much of their day sitting in. It may be a chair they've owned for years or, in our mother's case, a special chair they've bought for themselves in order to be more comfortable.

About six months before our mom went into long-term care, she purchased a lift chair from a well-known chain store that sells mobility aids. If you're not familiar with lift chairs, they are wonderful devices that raise and lower electronically in order to make sitting and getting out of the chair easier.

Buying this chair was such a great idea. If only we had been better educated before we made the purchase. *Please learn from our mistake.*

Since our mom wasn't mobile enough to come to the store with us, we had to buy the chair for her. We didn't realize that the depth of the seat cushion is of supreme importance. Our salesperson didn't tell us about this, so we wound up buying a model that was far too big for our mother's body. There was no question. We could not keep it.

Thankfully, the store manager agreed to refund our money – which was against store policy – and sold us a chair that was the proper size. If she hadn't had the compassion she did, we would have had to sell our mom's ill-fitting chair for a fraction of what she paid for it.

Survival Tip:

If you're buying a lift chair for your parent, be sure to take the measurements you need with you to the store. Measure your mom or dad (seated) from the base of their spine to the bend in their knee. This should be the approximate measurement of the depth of the chair's seat cushion. Be sure to ask the salesperson to work with you in order to get the best possible fit.

Time for a Wheelchair

A few months after the lift chair arrived, we had a meeting with our mom's occupational therapist at her supportive housing facility. Even though we knew this day was coming, we were surprised when he broke the news: Mom needed a wheelchair.

Our mother was terrified of being in a wheelchair. To her, it meant that the end was near. We did our best to reassure her that it was a wonderful development – something that would make her life so much easier.

She wasn't so sure.

The occupational therapist measured our mom and advised us on what kind of wheelchair would be best. In the end, we were able to borrow a chair from Mom's supportive housing home, and later borrowed one from her long-term care home as well. We were fortunate, and we knew it.

The occupational therapist also advised us that we'd need to rent a hospital bed and a commode chair from the healthcare company that he worked for. The bed was necessary because Mom needed siderails to ensure that she didn't fall onto the floor during the night. She also needed a bed that could be adjusted electronically for her own comfort. The commode chair was necessary, too. It stayed conveniently by her side so that she didn't have to walk to the bathroom.

As it turned out, these weren't the only speciality items that we needed. The OT (occupational therapist) also advised us to buy a ROHO cushion for our mother's lift chair and her wheelchair. Mom had bedsores and needed this special medical cushion that would offer some relief from the pressure and pain of being seated all day. ROHO is the Cadillac of cushions – specially engineered, filled with tiny air cells, and priced at an astonishing $600. We gulped. *Surely that must be a mistake*, we thought. It wasn't.

Survival Tip:

Wheelchairs, hospital beds, commodes and cushions are just a few of the assistive devices your parent may need. Take it from us: awareness is everything. Knowing now that you may need to rent or buy these things will make life easier for you later.

Assistive Devices Program

After we were told that our mom's cushion would cost $600, we asked the OT if the government would help us pay for it. That's when he told us about the ADP or

Assistive Devices Program, run by the province. Check out this link:

https://www.ontario.ca/page/mobility-aids

Here's the lowdown. The government will pay 75% of the cost of an approved assistive device. Who is eligible? Any Ontario resident who has a valid health card and who has been living with a physical disability for 6 months or longer.

According to the government, the program covers over 8,000 separate pieces of equipment or supplies, including:

- manual and power wheelchairs
- power scooters
- cushions, back and head supports, and other positioning devices
- oxygen supplies
- wheeled walkers
- prostheses

(The program does not help to cover the cost of renting these devices.)

In order to qualify, your parent must be examined by an occupational therapist or a physiotherapist who is registered with the program. That person must confirm that your mom or dad requires the mobility aid. They must also determine which type of aid best suits your parent's needs.

Not surprisingly, you have to be proactive here. It's up to you to email the program office and ask for a list of registered therapists in your area. Contact the ADP at: **adp@ontario.ca**

The next step is to choose a therapist and make an appointment. Visit the link below to print the application forms. Your parent's therapist will help you to fill them out.

http://www.forms.ssb.gov.on.ca/mbs/ssb/forms/ ssbforms.nsf/FormDetail?OpenForm&ACT= RDR&TAB=PROFILE&SRCH=1&ENV=W WE&TIT=4821&NO=014-2196-67E

[or http://bit.ly/2ZELmBU]

Finally, mail the completed forms to:

Assistive Devices Program
5700 Yonge Street, 7th Floor
Toronto, Ontario
M2M 4K5

The web page suggests the government will review the application within eight weeks of receiving it. The absurdity of this wasn't lost on us, of course. It's entirely possible that your dear mother or father might pass away before their application is given the green light. Unfortunately, that's life inside the system.

Survival Tip:

Don't purchase an assistive device before your ADP application is approved. If you buy one and your application is later denied, you're responsible for covering the whole cost. *Ouch.*

If your application is turned down, you'll receive a letter explaining the reason. The ADP office will also tell you how to appeal the decision.

If your application is approved, the government will contact your therapist, as well as the provider you've indicated you'd like to buy the device from. Arrangements will then be made to deliver the equipment to your home.

In our case, things just didn't work out. We contacted an approved therapist in order to apply to the ADP for the cushion that our mom needed. For some reason, our calls were never returned. After a few weeks, we gave up. Truth be told, we didn't have the energy to follow through.

Fortunately, there was a rainbow behind the clouds: we were able to buy a used cushion. We found one at a charitable organization in Niagara called Warehouse of Hope. It's a non-profit group dedicated to helping others at home and around the world by providing used medical equipment. Instead of potentially spending $150 (25% of $600), we found the perfect ROHO cushion in excellent condition for $30. Amazing.

Check out this link to **Warehouse of Hope**:

https://www.warehouseofhope.com/about_us

If you live outside the Niagara region, go online and research organizations that may exist near you. Trust us. A little homework now will pay off later.

Survival Tip:

Don't let the government paperwork involved in the Assistive Devices Program make you crazy. Take it one step at a time and ask your occupational therapist or physiotherapist to help you. It's their job to do so.

At the end of the day, buying or renting the assistive devices your parent needs doesn't have to be a stressful experience. Keep this chapter handy, and you'll have the guidance you need to get the job done.

Our Best Advice

"…I think I should like to go back to Kansas."

—Dorothy,
The Wonderful Wizard of Oz

11

Our Best Advice

"...I think I should like to go back to Kansas."

—Dorothy,
The Wonderful Wizard of Oz

We told you at the beginning of this book that you were about to start a journey down the yellow brick road... just like Dorothy in *The Wonderful Wizard of Oz*.

We warned that you'd see wicked witches and flying monkeys and munchkins at every turn. We said you may even feel like running home to Auntie Em and Uncle Henry. *Yikes!*

True to our word, we waved our magic wand over you every step of the way. You now have the survival tools you need to navigate the long-term care system much more smoothly than we ever did.

We would have given anything if someone had placed a book like this into our hands when we first started our journey. Months later, we recognized that we now had an opportunity to "pay it forward". The gift of caring for our mother gave us the knowledge and experience we needed to give this gift to you.

Before you head home to Kansas, here's a quick review of our best advice.

Love Yourself

Use the self-care strategies we suggested in the introduction and make your mental health a priority every day. Laugh, smile, breathe, and take care of you. Doing this will make all the difference.

Love yourself.

Be Proactive and Prepared

We know. It's human nature to avoid things that make you feel anxious or afraid. It's hard to accept that your elderly parent is not going to be with you forever. But until you face facts, you'll continue to procrastinate. It's one thing to put off writing a term paper in high school. It's another thing to put off preparing for one of the most challenging experiences of your adult life.

Looking back, we realize now that we should have begun our research long before our mother's health began to decline. Like some of you, we were in denial – hoping against hope that our mom might never need long-term care. The thing is, it doesn't always work out that way.

So don't just hope for the best. Take the bull by the horns, take charge, take action, and do it now.

Be proactive and prepared.

Be Organized

Remember the *Book of Verna*? It's so important that you approach your journey in an organized way. Your job as your parent's project manager is to document every conversation, every meeting and every tour. Whether you use a notebook or a Notes app, you will thank yourself later.

While you're at it, don't forget the camera on your phone. Take photos of the homes that you tour, and keep the pictures on your phone or computer for future reference. They'll come in handy when you're trying to remember the layout, features and benefits of each place. They'll also allow you to compare notes with friends who are doing research of their own.

Be organized.

Don't Settle

Finally, remember this. You are not at the mercy of the system. You have the power to get what you really want – so long as you're willing to put in the time and effort to educate yourself now. Don't settle for less than the best for your mother or father. They deserve it.

Don't settle.

Now grab those ruby slippers and get started.

EPILOGUE:
To All of You with Love

"A loving heart is the truest wisdom."

—Charles Dickens

EPILOGUE: To All of You with Love

"A loving heart is the truest wisdom."

—Charles Dickens

Love was the guiding light behind this book. We wrote it because of the love we felt and continue to feel for our mother, Verna.

We also wrote it because of the love we feel for all of you – and your mothers and fathers – who are going through this experience together.

We hope that we've helped you and your family to hang on to your collective sanity in the midst of what can be a trying and chaotic time.

Take heart: you are not alone.

Our sincere hope is that this book will be a trusted resource for you, a survival guide for one of the biggest adventures of your life.

It has been a privilege to share our stories and the lessons we've learned.

ACKNOWLEDGEMENTS

"Kindness is a language which the deaf
can hear and the blind can see."

—Mark Twain

ACKNOWLEDGEMENTS

"Kindness is a language which the deaf
can hear and the blind can see."

—Mark Twain

We would like to acknowledge the many people who showed kindness to us during our mother's journey through the long-term care system.

Thank you to the angels at Deer Park Villa in Grimsby.

Our deepest gratitude to the PSWs, nurses, doctors, staff and administrators at Upper Canada Lodge in Niagara-on-the-Lake. Because of you, the memories we have of our mother's final days are beautiful ones.

Thank you to the Hamilton Spectator for giving us the chance to tell our mother's story in May of 2019, and to raise awareness about the need to be proactive and prepared.

Finally, thank you to Verna Amelia Cumming for showing us how to embrace the end of life with such grace.

Your spirit lives on, Mom. Your family loves you so much.

BEFORE WE GO...

"Parting is such sweet sorrow..."

—William Shakespeare,
Romeo and Juliet

BEFORE WE GO…

"Parting is such sweet sorrow…"

—William Shakespeare,
Romeo and Juliet

We'd like to ask for your help before we go.

Now that you've read this little survival guide, we're wondering how the information inside of it may have helped you on your journey.

Would you please drop us a line? We'd love to share your feedback on our website to encourage others who may be stressed-out and struggling inside the system.

Send your comments and testimonials to: **indispensableguide@gmail.com.**

We can't wait to hear from you!

In the meantime, there's one more favour we'd like to ask.

Our goal is to reach as many Ontario baby boomers and seniors as we can with our message: *Be proactive and prepared.* From Windsor to Waterloo, Hamilton to Huntsville, Toronto to Timmins, and all the way down to Florida, Arizona and beyond… we need to spread the word.

Will you please help us? We'd be so grateful if you'd tell your friends, family and colleagues about this book and about the practical tips that it has to offer.

They can find *The Indispensable Survival Guide to Ontario's Long-Term Care System* in digital and print formats on Amazon.ca, chapters.indigo.ca, Kindle, Kobo and Smashwords.

Be sure to check our website regularly for an updated library of all the links to resources provided, the latest testimonials, social media links, and a blog designed to keep you informed of any changes to the system since the book's publication in 2019. You'll find us at **indispensableguide.ca**.

With heartfelt thanks,

Karen Cumming & Patricia Milne

APPENDIX:
Some Indispensable
Resources

"Alone we can do so little; together we can do so much."

—Helen Keller

APPENDIX: Some Indispensable Resources

> "Alone we can do so little; together we can do so much."
>
> —Helen Keller

Let's face it. We're all in this together. The more resources we can share with each other, the faster we'll get the job done.

Keep the following list of links and phone numbers handy. They'll make your journey down the long-term care yellow brick road that much easier.

Need the phone number for your local LHIN office?

The easiest way to find it is to Google the name of your LHIN and the words "phone number".

You could also call 2-1-1. This is a provincial helpline that offers information on community, social, health-related and government services. Operators can give you the phone number of your local LHIN, as well as pretty much any other number in the healthcare system. 2-1-1 is available 24 hours a day, 365 days a year. Amazingly, it provides an interpreter in over 150 languages.

We had no idea this existed.

Need to hire a PSW or a nurse privately?

There are a number of organizations that serve communities across Ontario and beyond. Here are a few of them:

AydCares has introduced a new way to book PSW care. It allows clients to use a mobile app in order to communicate with and book their preferred PSW directly.

For more information, call toll free: 1-800-293-6860, or consult the company's website:

https://www.aydcares.com/

Bayshore HealthCare offers a wide range of healthcare services for seniors across Canada. Call toll free: 1-844-877-3740, or click on the link below:

https://www.bayshore.ca/

Paramed also provides a variety of healthcare services for seniors nationwide. For more information visit:

https://www.paramed.com/our-locations/

Need emergency blood tests or other medical tests for your parent?

LifeLabs Mobile Lab Services makes house calls. In Ontario, call 1-877-849-3637, or visit:

https://www.lifelabs.com/tests-services/mobile-lab-services

Looking for information on dementia?

The Alzheimer Society of Ontario is an excellent resource:

https://alzheimer.ca/en/Home

In addition, check out this informative page on the **Canadian Institute for Health Information** website:

https://www.cihi.ca/en/dementia-in-canada/dementia-across-the-health-system/dementia-in-long-term-care

[or https://bit.ly/2ZrdmZF]

Got a complaint about your parent's long-term care facility?

Call the **Long-Term Care ACTION Line** toll-free: 1-866-434-0144, 8:30 a.m. to 7:00 p.m., 7 days a week.

Need to contact the Ministry of Health and Long-Term Care?

It was divided into two separate ministries in June of 2019. The Minister of Long-Term Care is the Honourable Merrilee Fullerton. If you have a question or concern, call the Ministry office at 416-327-4327 or toll-free at 1-800-268-1153.

Got a legal question?

Contact the **Advocacy Centre for the Elderly**. ACE is a community based legal clinic for low income seniors located in Toronto. It has lawyers on staff whose job it is to help seniors with questions about healthcare, elder abuse, consumer protection, wills, powers of attorney, etc. Its website is a very good source of legal information regarding long-term care. Call 416-598-2656 or visit:

http://www.advocacycentreelderly.org/

Looking for general information on long-term care?

Check out **The Ontario Long-Term Care Association**. The OLTCA is the largest association of long-term care providers in Canada. Its website is a good source of general info on the long-term care system. Reach them at 647-256-3490, or follow the link below for more info:

https://oltca.com/OLTCA/

Is your parent a veteran or the spouse of a veteran?

If so, they may qualify for government assistance to help pay for housekeeping services in supportive housing. They may also qualify for assistance to help pay for incontinence products in supportive housing. **Veterans Affairs** can be reached toll-free at 1-866-522-2122 or visit:

https://www.veterans.gc.ca/eng/health-support

Are you retired and in need of assistance?

The Canadian Association of Retired Persons (CARP) advocates for high quality healthcare for aging Canadians. If you'd like to bring a long-term care issue to CARP's attention, email **advocacy@carp.ca**.

Are you a snowbird?

The Canadian Snowbird Association is dedicated to defending and improving the rights and privileges of all Canadian travellers – many of whom are baby boomers with elderly parents. If you'd like to bring a long-term care issue to the CSA's attention, email them at **csastaff@snowbirds.org** or call toll-free: 1-800-265-3200.

ABOUT THE AUTHORS

Karen Cumming is a freelance journalist, health promoter and teacher who loves to help people manage their stress. She writes about mindful living, meditation and self-care at **karencumming.com**. Karen's background includes twenty years of reporting and producing for TV and radio, and more than a decade in the classroom. Her freelance features have appeared in the *Toronto Star*, the *Hamilton Spectator*, the *St. Catharines Standard* and the *Peterborough Examiner*.

Patricia Milne is a retired Early Childhood Educator, daughter, sister, wife, mother, grandmother, volunteer and traveller. She and her husband are snowbirds, spending their winters in a sunny community of like-minded and very active seniors. Patricia spent her career setting children up for success by teaching them to plan the steps of their daily tasks. As it turns out, planning is a valuable tool for success at any age... from childhood all the way through to long-term care.